HOCKEY
STRATEGIES

BY DAVID J. CLARKE

SportsZone

An Imprint of Abdo Publishing
abdobooks.com

abdobooks.com

Published by Abdo Publishing, a division of ABDO, PO Box 398166, Minneapolis, Minnesota 55439. Copyright © 2024 by Abdo Consulting Group, Inc. International copyrights reserved in all countries. No part of this book may be reproduced in any form without written permission from the publisher. SportsZone™ is a trademark and logo of Abdo Publishing.

Printed in the United States of America, North Mankato, Minnesota.
102023
012024

Cover Photo: David Zalubowski/AP Images
Interior Photos: Eliot J. Schechter/National Hockey League/Getty Images, 5, 41; Maddie Meyer, Getty Images Sport/Getty Images, 6–7; China Wong/National Hockey League/Getty Images, 9; Bardocz Peter/Shutterstock Images, 10; Jared Silber/National Hockey League/Getty Images, 13, 16–17; Steve Babineau/National Hockey League/Getty Images, 14; Andrew Mordzynski/Icon Sportswire/Getty Images, 19; Bruce Bennett/Getty Images Sport/Getty Images, 21; Ethan Miller/Getty Images Sport/Getty Images, 22–23; Christopher Mast/National Hockey League/Getty Images, 24; David Becker/National Hockey League/Getty Images, 26–27; Zak Krill/National Hockey League/Getty Images, 29; John McCreary/Icon Sportswire/Getty Images, 30; Fred Kfoury III/Icon Sportswire/Getty Images, 33; Jim MacIsaac/Getty Images Sport/Getty Images, 36–37; Len Redkoles/National Hockey League/Getty Images, 39; Harrison Barden/Getty Images Sport/Getty Images, 44–45

Editor: Steph Giedd
Series Designer: Joshua Olson

Library of Congress Control Number: 2023939424

Publisher's Cataloging-in-Publication Data

Names: Clarke, David J., author.
Title: Hockey strategies / by David J. Clarke
Description: Minneapolis, Minnesota: Abdo Publishing, 2024 | Series: Sports strategies | Includes online resources and index.
Identifiers: ISBN 9781098292454 (lib. bdg.) | ISBN 9798384910398 (ebook)
Subjects: LCSH: Sports teams--Juvenile literature. | Teamwork (Sports)--Juvenile literature. | Athletes--Training of--Juvenile literature. | Hockey--Juvenile literature.
Classification: DDC 796.01--dc23

TABLE OF CONTENTS

INTRODUCTION

Hockey's end-to-end action can look like chaos. Playing inside a fully enclosed arena, skaters zoom around the ice at speeds of up to 25 miles per hour (40 km/h). And while individual moments of skill and flair can make a play happen, many big moments come down to careful planning.

On the forecheck, a team can pursue the puck in many ways. Some teams swarm the opposing defense, looking for quick turnovers. Others sit back, hoping to spring traps on the opposition in the neutral zone.

The term *special teams* in hockey refers to the power play and penalty kill. On a power play, a team must find creative ways to make use of its extra players. Those players also must find a way to unlock a penalty kill unit. The unit's only job is to defend tightly. The players on the ice for the shorthanded team try their best to cover the space.

If a National Hockey League (NHL) game goes to overtime, everything changes. The introduction of 3-on-3 play opens up the ice and brings the need for an entirely new set of tactics. And if the game doesn't end there, success in a shootout at the end of the season could be the difference between a playoff berth and an early summer.

Members of the Florida Panthers, *in red*, and Vegas Golden Knights battle for a face-off during Game 4 of the 2023 Stanley Cup Final.

MARTINEZ
23
BARKOV
16
REINHART
13
KARLSSON
71
LUNDELL
15

CHAPTER 1

FORECHECKING AND BACKCHECKING

The Florida Panthers were on the verge of a stunning upset in the first round of the 2023 Stanley Cup playoffs. The Panthers were facing a Boston Bruins team that had won an NHL-record 65 games during the regular season. Boston then raced out to a 3–1 series lead. However, the Panthers battled back to force Game 7. And trailing 3–2 with a minute to play, Florida defenseman Brandon Montour scored to force overtime.

The Panthers came out aggressively in the extra session. Just over nine minutes in, a Florida player dumped the puck into

Florida's Carter Verhaeghe, *right*, and Boston's Taylor Hall battle for the puck during the teams' opening-round playoff series in 2023.

the Boston zone. Panthers winger Matthew Tkachuk raced in after it. But he wasn't alone. Linemate Sam Bennett joined him behind the Boston net.

The pair outdueled two Boston defenders for the puck. Eventually Bennett dug it free from a crowd of skates. He turned and passed the puck to the Panthers third forward, Carter Verhaeghe, who was wide-open in front of the net. Verhaeghe ripped a shot past Boston goalie Jeremy Swayman to win the game and the series. Boston's historic season ended with a thud because the Panthers were willing to take a chance.

RISK VS. REWARD

Although forechecking happens in the offensive zone, it is a defensive tactic in hockey. It happens only when a team does not have possession of the puck. Winning the puck back is one goal of a good forecheck. But there are other ways to determine if a forecheck is successful.

A play like the one Tkachuk, Bennett, and Verhaeghe made to win the series against Boston is the best-case scenario for a forechecking team. Attacking the opposing defensemen before they can make a decision is a great way to cause turnovers right away. And those turnovers can lead to easy goals.

In many cases, however, a team cannot get to the defensive puck carrier that quickly. If they can't, the next best thing is

The Florida Panthers celebrate Verhaeghe's Game 7 overtime goal to upset the Bruins.

to make sure that the puck carrier does not have easy options for moving up the ice. Good forechecking teams do this by staying organized.

Teams use many forechecking formations. Most teams use some variation of three alignments—the 1-2-2, the 2-1-2, and the 1-3-1. In all three, the first number represents the players who will be attacking the puck carrier deep in the offensive zone. The more people a team has on the front line generally means a more aggressive forecheck. The middle number is the second line of players. They are there to support the main forecheckers. The third number represents the players who will stay back to prevent long breakaway passes.

1-2-2 Forecheck

In a 1-2-2 forecheck, F1 attacks the puck carrier as soon as the carrier takes possession. Then, once the puck is passed, F1, F2, and F3 scramble to cover the other passing options. D1 and D2 shift to overload the side of the ice that the puck is on. That way the team with possession cannot move up the ice quickly.

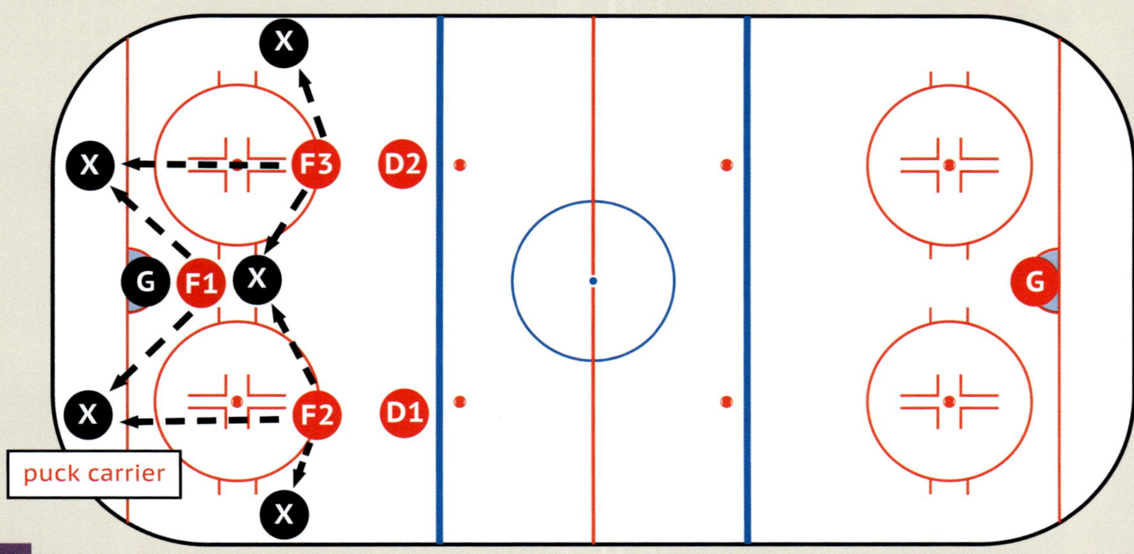

If the first line of forecheckers can't win the puck, its next job is to make sure the opposing puck carrier can't make a clean pass. The second line of forecheckers helps by cutting off potential receivers. If the opposing defenseman has no options, he might simply dump the puck out of the zone. Then the forechecking team's defenders can retrieve it, and their team has possession again.

KNOWING THE SITUATION

Forechecking strategies can be adjusted for a variety of reasons. All teams have a preferred forechecking strategy. But there are times when a team must be more or less aggressive.

A team that is killing a penalty is not likely to forecheck deep in the offensive zone. It doesn't have enough players to do so effectively. A team that has a lead late in the game is also more likely to sit back in the neutral zone. Since forechecking leaves space behind a team's defense, sending too many players up the ice can be risky. Late in games, the team with the lead might pull its first line of forecheckers back to the offensive blue line or even the center red line. The defending team can sit back and then apply pressure once the opponent with the puck gets to that area.

Trying to pull off the upset against Boston, Florida played the aggressive style it had all year. During the 2022–23 regular season, only the Carolina Hurricanes scored more goals off forechecking plays than the Panthers did. That aggressiveness was the reason Florida made the playoffs. And it was also the reason the team was moving to the second round.

GETTING BACK

One of the terms coaches and scouts love to use to describe hardworking hockey players is "200-foot" players. That means they work hard to cover the entire 200-foot length of the ice. It's a reputation many players strive for. And players can't earn it if they don't get back on defense—what is known as "backchecking."

If forechecking fails to create a turnover, the defensive team must get back and cover. Its new job is to stay in front of the rushing opposition. This isn't always as easy as it sounds. Since hockey is a fluid game, players can maneuver all over the ice. And since teams change lines during the action, new players can appear on the ice at any time.

Detroit Red Wings captain Dylan Larkin, *right*, is considered a "200-foot" player because he's strong on both offense and defense.

The first job of a backchecking team is to slow the puck down. The defender closest to the puck carrier must deny a clean path to the net. As the play enters the defending team's zone, the closest defender will try to force the puck carrier to the outside and away from dangerous scoring areas.

Patrice Bergeron, *right*, of the Boston Bruins won his NHL-record sixth Selke Trophy in 2022–23. The award is given to the best defensive forward every season.

The rest of the defenders then drop back and pick up the puck carrier's passing options. That is relatively easy if the teams have even numbers. But if the offensive team outnumbers the defenders, such as a 2-on-1 or a 3-on-2, the defenders need to adjust. In that case, the defenders must cut off the passing lanes. Defenders can't let the puck carrier skate straight in on goal. But their main job is to not allow the puck carrier an easy pass across the ice, which can lead to a good scoring opportunity.

Hockey is free-flowing and often played in transition. But having a plan to deal with the unexpected is important for any team. The team that can control the opposition on the backcheck can shut down a good offense. And a team that can forecheck can effectively give itself great chances to score. In Florida's case, it allowed the Panthers to stun the NHL world and make a run all the way to the Stanley Cup Final.

CHAPTER 2

OFFENSE AND DEFENSE

Having a strategy and executing it aggressively can be the difference between a good hockey team and a great one. A team's ability to create turnover opportunities on defense and then turn them into scoring opportunities is critical. That showed when the New Jersey Devils and New York Rangers met in a 2023 first-round playoff series.

The teams have long had a fierce rivalry. Regular-season games between the neighbors are often heated battles. The temperature rises even higher when they

Ondřej Palát, *right*, of the New Jersey Devils battles for a loose puck with the New York Rangers' Vladimir Tarasenko during the teams' 2023 playoff series.

meet in the playoffs. In 2023 the series went to a decisive Game 7. Everything was on the line.

With six minutes to play, the Devils held a 2–0 lead. But the Rangers had the puck in the offensive zone. The Devils had played aggressively on defense all game. That continued as the Rangers tried to work the puck along the right wall. As the New York players attempted to find space, three Devils closed in. Eventually, New Jersey winger Ondřej Palát poked the puck free. Palát was instantly tied up, but linemate Jack Hughes came in for support. He gained control of the puck and went streaking up the ice.

The pressing Rangers were caught. They had only one defender back as Hughes and Erik Haula broke into the offensive zone. Hughes charged up the left wing and then flipped a pass over the defenseman's stick. It landed perfectly on Haula's blade. In one motion, the Finnish center hammered the puck past Rangers goalie Igor Shesterkin for a 3–0 lead. The Devils were well on their way to the next round. And they had just showed how quickly aggressive defense can lead to offense in hockey.

FINDING SPACE

Though much of hockey is played in transition, there are also many times when a team is set up in the offensive zone.

Erik Haula, *left*, and Jack Hughes celebrate after Haula's goal in Game 7 against the Rangers.

Then hockey becomes a chess match. The five offensive players must find a way to create room to score. And since they can't let the puck cross the blue line without putting teammates offside, space is tight.

With limited room in which to work, offenses have to get creative to open up defenses and create scoring opportunities. Cycling is something that all offenses do. Cycling involves three or more players constantly moving and passing the puck, usually in a circular or triangular pattern. The idea is to keep themselves and the puck moving. That way the defenders have to keep chasing. The more moving a defensive team has to do, the more likely it is to break down and allow the attacking team an open scoring chance.

Another option for the offense is to create traffic in front of the net. Highlight goals often come off flashy rushes up the ice. But a team needs to be able to grind out chances on scramble plays too. Getting bodies to the front of the net can give a team chances to score off rebounds. Additionally, big, strong forwards stationed in front can make it tough for goalies to see shots.

The Detroit Red Wings were one of the best teams in the NHL in the 1990s and 2000s. One of their key players was winger Tomas Holmström. The Swede wasn't Detroit's best player. But he was 6 feet tall and 200 pounds. Holmström was famous for parking himself in front of goalies and making their lives miserable. He scored 243 career goals, often on rebounds and deflections. His ability to screen goalies helped defensemen such as Nicklas Lidström and Brian Rafalski

Detroit Red Wings winger Tomas Holmström hoists the Stanley Cup after his team defeated the Pittsburgh Penguins in six games in 2008.

become high scorers as well. Holmström was a part of four Stanley Cup championships between 1997 and 2008.

DEFENSIVE LOCKDOWN

Defending teams must choose how aggressively they want to play in their own end. Some teams form a tight shell around the net to keep opposing offenses out of what are

PANTHERS
72
EKBLAD
5
13
REINHART
20

called "high-danger" scoring areas. This is an effective strategy for keeping the best chances at bay. But it can also prevent defending teams from getting the puck back quickly.

Other teams want to pressure offenses and force mistakes. If done well, playing this way can both frustrate offenses and create turnovers. Many times those turnovers can become odd-man rushes heading the other way. But if a team makes a mistake playing this way, the puck could end up in the back of its own net.

When teams set up defensively, their alignment often looks like the letter X. Two wingers play up high from the top of the face-off circles to the blue line. Two defensemen form the bottom points of the X, playing near the net. The center plays in the middle, linking the two lines together.

Aaron Ekblad, *left*, Sam Reinhart, *center*, and Aleksander Barkov, *right*, of the Florida Panthers crowd the crease to assist goaltender Sergei Bobrovsky.

Defenders often try to close down space and force offensive players to give up the puck.

How teams play out of that formation changes, however. Some teams play man-to-man defense. The two wingers cover the other team's defensemen at the point, which is the area just inside the blue line. The defensemen cover the forwards near the net. The center takes the fifth player.

Other teams will play zone defense. Players are responsible for the areas of the ice where they line up. Teams that play this way need to communicate well to make sure a teammate is aware of an offensive player moving into his or her area.

Aggressive teams might play like the Devils did against New York, which is called an overload. The side of the ice the puck is on is called the strong side. An overload defense will attack the puck, usually by moving three players to swarm that side of the ice. The idea is to create a quick turnover by forcing a puck carrier to make a play in a crowd.

The problem with overloading the strong side of the ice is that it leaves space on the opposite, or weak, side. If an offensive player can work free of an overload's pressure, he will likely have teammates moving into wide-open spaces. That can lead to very good scoring chances.

CHAPTER 3

SPECIAL TEAMS

The Edmonton Oilers entered the second period of Game 4 of their 2023 playoff series against the Los Angeles Kings in big trouble. Edmonton was already down 2–1 in the series, and the first period of the fourth game had been a disaster. The Oilers were trailing 3–0 in Los Angeles.

Just over three minutes into the second period, the Kings committed a tripping penalty. That meant Edmonton would have an extra skater while Los Angeles defenseman Alex Edler was in the penalty box. As the Oilers' power play was winding

Leon Draisaitl of the Edmonton Oilers led the NHL in power play goals with 32 during the 2022–23 season.

down, Edmonton's Leon Draisaitl controlled the puck along the right wall. He flipped a pass to defenseman Evan Bouchard at the blue line. Bouchard moved the puck to Connor McDavid on the left side. McDavid quickly whipped it back across the ice to Draisaitl on the right wing.

By that point, the Kings' defensemen were completely disorganized. The Oilers' puck movement was so quick that the Kings were scrambling all over the ice. Draisaitl once again passed the puck to Bouchard out near the blue line. The right-handed shooting defenseman stepped into the puck and unloaded a hard slap shot past two defenders and into the net.

The goal sparked an Edmonton comeback. By the end of the second period, the Oilers had scored twice more. One of the other goals also came on a power play. Edmonton eventually won the game 5–4 in overtime. The Oilers went on to win the series in six games.

POWER TRIO

The Edmonton Oilers' history-making power play in the 2023 playoffs featured the NHL's three top power play scorers in 2022–23. Connor McDavid led the league with 71 power play points. Leon Draisaitl was second with 62, and center Ryan Nugent-Hopkins had 53. Only two players on the other 31 NHL teams topped 40 power play points during the season.

Players with hard, accurate slap shots from the blue line, such as Edmonton's Evan Bouchard, can be dangerous power play weapons in the NHL.

THE MAN ADVANTAGE

Most of a hockey game is played five-on-five, also known as even strength. But when penalties occur, one team ends up on the penalty kill. The other has a power play. Together, these are known as hockey's "special teams."

Alex Ovechkin of the Washington Capitals became the league's all-time power play scoring leader in December 2021.

The first thing an offensive team must do on a power play is establish possession. The easiest way to do that is by winning the initial face-off. But if the defensive team gains control of the puck and clears it, the full-strength team has to find a way to get the puck back into the offensive zone. Teams hope to do that by carrying the puck in, since that keeps it in their possession. But often the defensive team will post all four players near its own blue line to stop this. In that case, an offensive team might dump the puck in and use their extra man to try to win the race for it.

Once set up, different power plays attack in different ways. Some teams prefer to crowd the net and screen goalies. Others try to spread the ice to make defenders cover more ground. By getting defenders to move, the offense hopes to open passing lanes and set up easier shots. An overload power play might put four players toward one side of the ice, forcing a defense to move bodies that way. Then the fifth player might be open for a backdoor pass. A 1-3-1 power play gets one player in the slot, which is the area between the face-off circles. He tries to occupy the four defenders and open up space for teammates. But he can also be a passing option. Pucks played to him can turn into quick, high-quality shots or even quicker passes to a teammate. That player is often referred to as the bumper because of how quickly that player gets rid of the puck.

What the Oilers used to score against the Kings is called an "umbrella" power play. It features one player at the blue line, in the center of the ice. Then two players line up on either wing, near the half-wall, which is the area along the boards roughly halfway between the blue line and the goal line. The other two forwards maneuver near the net.

The three players up high, near the blue line, try to do exactly what Bouchard, Draisaitl, and McDavid did. They move the puck quickly and hope to make the defense race around to cover any potential shooters. When a hole opens, a player can shoot. The two players near the net are ideally placed for screens and rebounds. If the puck bounces free behind the net, the offensive players can also quickly retrieve it and get it back to the three players up high.

The Oilers used this strategy to put together the best single-season power play numbers in NHL history in 2022–23. Edmonton scored on 32.4 percent of its chances during the season. Only three other NHL teams had ever cracked 30 percent. The last team to do so was the 1978–79 New York Islanders.

ON THE KILL

When one team has an extra skater on the power play, the other team is shorthanded. They try to keep the clock moving until their teammate gets out of the penalty box. That's called penalty killing, and it is stressful work. Penalty killers need to stay disciplined. They can't chase the puck, because one mistake can leave far too much open space behind them.

Brad Marchand, *left*, tries to take away an opponent's shooting lane while killing a penalty for the Boston Bruins.

They might also have to block shots. But in doing so, they need to avoid screening their own goalie. A missed block and a screened goalie often lead to an opposing goal.

There are many ways to set up a four-man penalty kill. One is a passive box. In this setup, the four penalty killers form a tight square around the slot. The goal is to keep the puck to the outside or up at the point. Any players who come close to the net can be crowded out by the defenders. And defenders are also taught to keep their sticks on the ice to deflect passes.

Some teams will play a more aggressive box. Two players, usually defensemen, stay down low. But the other two players might pressure the sides and up high more often. They try to make offensive players rush their passes, which could lead to mistakes or even interceptions. With the right break, a defender might be able to race the other way for a shorthanded scoring opportunity. But as with any aggressive play in hockey, this carries a risk of leaving open space behind.

Another popular formation is the diamond. One defenseman stays in the low slot. The other defenseman moves up to form the sides of the diamond with one of the forwards. The other forward positions up top, near the blue line. Like the

THE DROP

In recent years, many hockey teams have tried what is called "the drop" to carry the puck into the offensive zone. To do it, one player will race from behind his own net with the puck. His aim is to back the defense up. Once he gets to the center red line or feels any pressure, he drops the puck back to a trailing teammate. Since this player has a full head of steam moving onto the pass, he is harder to stop from entering the zone.

large box, the diamond is designed to be more aggressive. Often the two are used together, depending on where the puck moves.

Sometimes a team has to kill two penalties at once. The team is two players shorthanded. In that case, the three defenders will line up in a triangle. In a 5-on-3 situation, the defending team is only trying to keep players out of the middle of the ice. The three players bunch close to the net. Most of the time, offensive teams can pass the puck around the outside against three defenders without having to worry about pressure.

The goalie's role becomes even more important when killing penalties. Since the team does not have enough players to cover everyone on offense, the player with the puck is often the goalie's sole focus. The goalie tracks the puck wherever it goes, anticipating a potential shot. Goalies need to be especially alert in a 5-on-3 situation.

Special teams are often some of the most exciting parts of a game. And the strategic battle between the offense and defense often brings fans to the edges of their seats. That's for good reason. Whichever team wins these special teams battles often wins the game.

OVERTIME AND SHOOTOUTS

Philadelphia Flyers goalie Brian Boucher stared down New York Rangers center Olli Jokinen on April 11, 2010. The crowd at Wachovia Center in Philadelphia was on its feet. It was the last day of the regular season, and Philadelphia's Claude Giroux had just scored to put the Flyers up 2–1 in a shootout. If Boucher could stop Jokinen, Philadelphia would win the game.

However, there was so much more on the line. The two teams were tied in the standings with 86 points.

Philadelphia's Brian Boucher, *left*, stops New York's Olli Jokinen to win a shootout on April 11, 2010, and send the Flyers to the playoffs.

Each team had already earned one point because the game went to overtime. But the second point, given to the winner of the game, made all the difference. The winner of this game was headed to the playoffs. The loser was headed home.

Jokinen started from his own end and sprinted up the ice. He gathered the puck on his stick with speed and moved in on Boucher before dekeing to his backhand. Jokinen was trying to get Boucher's legs to open up. That way the Finnish forward could hit a shot through the five hole, between the goalie's legs. But Boucher squeezed his pads together and stuffed the attempt.

The Flyers' goalie threw his hands in the air as the fans went crazy. Philadelphia was in the playoffs. And the Flyers made the most of it. Their run didn't stop until they were beaten by the Chicago Blackhawks in a six-game Stanley Cup Final. None of that would have happened without winning the dramatic final-day shootout.

A CHANGE IN THE RULES

Just 10 years earlier, that exciting moment would not have happened at all. From 1942 to 1983, any NHL regular-season game tied at the end of three periods stayed that way. Each team received one point in the standings. A five-minute overtime was added in the 1983–84 regular season. The winner

Boucher, *center*, is congratulated by center Jeff Carter, *left*, and backup goalie Sébastien Caron after the Flyers' victory over the Rangers.

in overtime got two points, and the losing team got none. But at the end of five minutes, if the score was still tied, both teams went home with one point.

But after 15 years with that system, something became clear: Each team would rather have had one point than none. It wasn't worth risking the one point they already had to try for the victory. So the NHL changed the rules again in 1999–2000. Teams would no longer lose the one point in overtime. But the winning team would still get two. In 2005–06 the league went one step further. It introduced the shootout and eliminated ties completely.

Shootout strategy is simple. Each team selects three skaters to take penalty shots. A skater gets one chance to put his best dekes or shots on a goalie. The only rules are that the skater cannot stop his forward skating momentum, and he must score on the first shot—no rebound goals are allowed. Whichever team has scored more after the three rounds wins

Nick Bjugstad, *right*, of the Florida Panthers moves in on Washington Capitals goalie Braden Holtby in the 20th round of a shootout in a 2014 game between the two teams. Bjugstad scored on the play to end the longest shootout in NHL history.

the game. If it is still tied, the shootout continues with sudden death rounds. New shooters are chosen each round, and the shootout continues until a round is completed in which one team scores and the other does not.

Not all fans liked it. Some thought it was a gimmicky way to end a game. But coaches knew it could mean a big boost in the standings. They had to plan for how to win shootouts.

All teams quickly identified their best shooters. They weren't always the top offensive players on each team. The Rangers' first shooter in that April 2010 game was Erik Christensen. The forward wasn't a superstar. But he was a shootout ace. In 55 career attempts, he scored 29 times. That 52.7 percent rate is the highest of any NHL player with more than 50 career shots.

Coaches also quickly learned which goalies they could trust in shootouts. Again, they weren't always the superstars. Sometimes even the best goalies aren't strong on breakaways. Of goalies who have faced at least 40 career shootout shots,

the best shootout goalie ever was journeyman Marc Denis.
He had a career record of 112–179–31 in 11 seasons with four
teams. But he stopped 36 of his 41 shootout attempts for a save
percentage of 85.4. The winningest goalie of all time, Martin
Brodeur, stopped only 69.3 percent of his shootout attempts.

OVERTIME EXCITEMENT

When the NHL changed its rules in 1999, it also made overtime
4-on-4. The idea was to create more room on the ice. The
added space led to more scoring opportunities, which meant
the game was less likely to go on to a shootout.

In 2015–16 NHL overtime was reduced to 3-on-3. With even
more space for each player, overtime sessions became truly
wide-open. It also completely changed the strategy. With four
players on the ice, two players went forward and two stayed
back. But with only three, everyone needs to create offense.
Any misplaced pass is likely an odd-man rush the other way.

With that in mind, possession of the puck means everything
in overtime. That changes the way players operate. Instead of
trying a tricky pass, a player often holds on to the puck and
cycles it again to make sure his receiver is truly open.

During regulation, offensive teams fight hard to keep
the puck in the offensive zone. Losing the zone means four
teammates must skate back to center ice and regroup, or else

they will be trapped offside. In overtime, players will often rush up the ice to try an attack. But if it looks as if they are skating into a spot that will cause a turnover, they will simply skate back out again and reload.

In the 3-on-3 format, smooth-skating star players are often the overtime heroes. In 2022–23 the Colorado Avalanche won nine overtime games. Three overtime-winning goals were scored by star winger Mikko Rantanen. Center Nathan MacKinnon, the team's top scorer, and superstar defenseman Cale Makar each had two. With the help of those nine extra wins, plus six more in shootouts, the Avalanche tipped the Dallas Stars by one point to win the Central Division title.

Devon Toews, *left*, and Mikko Rantanen of the Colorado Avalanche celebrate after Rantanen's overtime winning goal against the Montreal Canadiens in December 2022.

GLOSSARY

dekeing
Faking out an opponent.

even strength
Teams have equal numbers of players on the ice.

face-off
Dropping a puck between one player from each team to restart play.

forecheck
When the team without the puck applies pressure in the offensive zone to try to regain possession.

journeyman
A player who has played for many teams but isn't a star.

neutral zone
The area between the two blue lines.

penalty kill
When a team must play down a man while a player serves a suspension in the penalty box.

points
The total number of goals and assists a player accumulates in a season.

power play
Having more players on the ice than the opponent because of a penalty.

screen
To obstruct the view of the goalie.

shorthanded
Playing with one skater fewer due to a penalty.

slap shot
A hard and fast shot with a long backswing and powerful follow-through.

Books

Davidson, B. Keith. *NHL*. New York: Crabtree Publishing, 2022.

Flynn, Brendan. *Hockey*. Minneapolis, MN: Abdo Publishing, 2023.

Hewson, Anthony K. *GOATs of Hockey*. Minneapolis, MN: Abdo Publishing, 2022.

Online Resources

To learn more about hockey strategies, please visit **abdobooklinks.com** or scan this QR code. These links are routinely monitored and updated to provide the most current information available.

INDEX

ABOUT THE AUTHOR

David J. Clarke is a freelance sportswriter. Originally from Helena, Montana, he now lives in Savannah, Georgia, with his golden retriever, Gus.